TABLE OF CONTENTS

## Introduction to the MacBook Air 2020

The MacBook Air 2020 runs on the new macOS Catalina 10.15 with updates to existing apps plus and new feature additions like Apple music, Apple TV, Sidecar and Find My. MacBook Air 2020 has an Integrated Touch ID sensor and Retina display. The device is fitted with an 8-core processor, a new thermal design and up to 16 GB of memory.

The MacBook Air is secured with Apple's T2 Security Chip which enables the device to boot securely and encrypt the storage capabilities.

The Retina display feature empowers the MacBook to deliver amazing true-to-life pictures (over 4 million pixels) with the brilliant 500 nits brightness capability.

The MacBook Air also features a new scissor switch keyboard with more space between each key that delivers a surreal, comfortable typing experience, six-speaker sound system, longer battery life and Force Touch Trackpad.

The new Advanced Thermal Design includes a fan design that allows an increased airflow and heat disposal mechanism. These developments make the MacBook cool faster and run at higher power and workloads for extended periods of time.

The MacBook Air 2020 has a 13.3 inch and is fitted with Intel's 10$^{th}$ generation processors with speeds up to 3.8 GHz. Students, Arcade Gamers, Software / App Developers, Photographers, Filmmakers, Music Producers, Researchers and other professionals who desire a high productivity machine will find the device very useful for comprehensive, world-class output whether it is code writing and compilation, model simulations, gaming, photo video and music editing.

The MacBook Air 2020 is powered by a 49.9Wh lithium-polymer battery that delivers up to 13 hours of battery life. The new sidecar feature allows users to utilize their iPad as a second screen. Quick access to files is possible using the Gallery view in Finder.

Overall, exploit the power, amazing design and productivity your MacBook Air 2020 is capable of by reading this guide to fully optimize usage of the device.

**Unboxing: What's in the Package**

The Apple MacBook Air 2020 comes in the familiar Apple packaging and contains the following items

- MacBook Air 2020.
- USB-C Charge Cable to transfer data and charge the MacBook.
- 30W Power Adapter which once connected to the USB-C Charge Cable and plugged into an AC power outlet, charges the Mac

Be sure to read the safety information and usage instructions in the following pages carefully before you power the device or connect to a power outlet via cable.

## Getting Started with the MacBook Air 2020

After unboxing your new MacBook Air, the next thing you need to do is to setup the device. The MacBook Air is easy to use and was designed for a quick set up. You can start using the Mac by utilizing the information contained in following pages as a guide to complete the process

- Plug in the power adapter, connect the cables and charge the device
- Power on the MacBook Air
- User account and settings configuration including using the setup assistant

## How to Plug in the power adapter, connect the cables and charge the device

Remove the film material around the power adapter. The film is intended as a protective cover around the adapter to prevent it from damage.

Next, the AC plug with the USB cable fixed into it should be inserted into a power outlet and the other end of the cable should be inserted into the power adapter port of the MacBook Air. (Ensure the power ratings of the plug and the power outlet are compatible to avoid damaging the device). It is important to ensure the device is charging so that it does not shut down unexpectedly or run out of battery during the setup process.

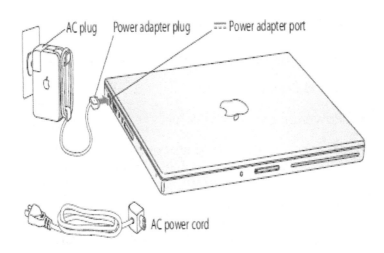

AC plug    Power adapter plug    ⸬ Power adapter port

AC power cord

Lift the lid of the Mac and boot the device. The battery charge status icon at the right of the menu bar indicates the battery level and charging status A battery charging icon shows that the MacBook is well connected to the AC source. The battery charges faster when the MacBook is off or in a sleep mode. Once the battery is

6

fully charged, please remove the cable and disconnect the AC plug from the power outlet.

For optimal usage of the battery and to conserve the battery power, disconnect any accessories connected to the Mac that are not in use, reduce the display brightness and close any unused apps. Also, the energy saver preferences (access these settings from System Preferences) allows you to change your power settings to suit your needs at any time.

For more information on how to get the most juice out of your MacBook Air 2020 battery and its usage span, please visit (https://www.apple.com/batteries/)

Charging          Charged

**How to Power on the MacBook Air**

Briefly press the power button ⏻ until there is a display on the screen which implies that the device is coming on. Be careful not to press the power button for too long as a long press may cause the device to go off. When the computer is on, the sleep indicator light also comes on and an audible unmistakable tone is heard during the booting.

**How to Configure User Accounts and Other Settings (including the setup assistant)**

Once the computer is fully on, the sleep indicator light goes off and the setup assistant is auto-activated. The setup assistant was built as a walkthrough guide for the first steps required to use the MacBook Air. To select, click, double-click and move items around on the screen, use the trackpad.

Choose your **Country** and click **Continue**. You can change this later by navigating to **System Preferences > Language and Region.**

Next, pick the Keyboard layout of your choice and click **Continue**. Choose your **network type** (Wi-Fi, Ethernet or none and click continue). Select your preferred Internet Protocol (IP) from the connection type list and enter the IP address, subnet mask, default gateway and DNS server address in the required fields and then click **Continue**. If there are available Wi-Fi networks available, just select your Wi-Fi network and enter the passcode to connect to the Internet through the network.

Apple's Data and Privacy Information comes up on the screen. The information would help you understand how Apple makes use of the data it collects from you as you use the MacBook Air 2020 especially in terms of product improvement and research focused on future updates. Read through the information and click **Continue**.

To transfer Information to this MacBook, select the right option from the available options like From a Mac, Time Machine Backup, startup disk or from a windows PC. If you do not have existing Data to transfer or would prefer to do this later, select the option **Don't transfer any Information now.**

Enter your **Apple ID** in the required field, click **Continue** and input the corresponding password. If you do not already have one, you can create one during this set-up. After getting an Apple ID, you can then sign in to your device.  The Apple ID is very important, and it comprises of an email address and a password. Just one Apple ID is required to use any Apple Service and it is best practice not to share the details with anyone. Apple ID is the account that will enable you get the most out of your Apple devices - including downloading apps from the App Store, Siri, Touch ID, buying music and movies from iTunes Store, pushing and storing content in iCloud and other Apple resources.

If the password you entered is correct, you will be automatically signed into apps and services that require Apple ID. If you do not remember your Apple ID password, click on the **'Forgot Apple ID or password?'** link that is available in the sign in window for the recovery of the password.

The Terms and Conditions window contains license terms for using the Apple device that you need to read and click **Agree**.

Input all the compulsory fields and then click on **Create a Computer Account window** and then **Continue**.

Congratulations! You have created a new user account with which you can log into your MacBook Air with admin rights allowing you to download and install apps, create other user accounts and make system changes.

Next, configure your device with frequently used settings by clicking **Continue** on the Express SetUp

11

window. This takes you to the Desktop screen page and the setup is complete.

### Check for Software Updates

Once the setup is completed, locate the **Finder or Dock** and click on App Store. Select **find and install any software updates** to find out and install any available software updates. You can begin to use your Mac once your software is up to date.

### Getting to know your MacBook Air

This section will take you on a tour of your Mac aimed at guiding and providing you with a basic anatomy of the device to learn what the different parts are, useful for and where they are located.

### Desktop

Once the computer boots, the landing page is the desktop where basic functions such as opening apps, searching for and organizing files and documents. Basically, once you are at the Desktop, you can navigate to find any files, app or folder and access any functionality of your choice.

Help menu | Menu bar | Wi-Fi | Spotlight

Finder | Dock | System Preferences

**Dock**

The Dock is a panel (located by default at the bottom of the screen that) stores all the frequently used and active (in use) apps, files and folders for quick and easy access. Though by default the Dock is positioned along the lower portion of the screen, you can also decide the new positioning and also the arrangement of the shortcuts in the Dock except that of Finder and Trash. You can also have the Dock hidden automatically when you are not using it.

To change the position of the Dock, go to **System Preferences > Dock** and select whether you want the pock to be placed on the **Left, Bottom** or **Right**.

To add apps to the dock, click on **Finder,** then **Applications** and next select the desired App and drag it to the Dock and release the hold on the app while it is on the Dock. You can also right click on a running app's icon in the Dock, select **Options** in the list of menus and select **Keep in Dock.**

To save files and folders to the Dock, click on **Finder,** then select the desired file or folder and drag it to the Dock (right hand side) and release the hold on the app

To remove an app, file or folder from the Dock, select the item and drag to the desktop. The option to remove will appear above the item and once you release the drag action, the item will no longer be available on the Dock.

The size of the Dock can be adjusted to make the icons larger or smaller on the screen. This can be achieved by clicking on the **Apple menu,** selecting '**System Preferences'**, next the **Dock** and moving the Size slider to the left or right. You can also automatically hide and show the Dock by ticking the box for **Automatically hide and show the Dock.**

To hide applications your recently accessed from the Dock, go to system preferences, open the dock and check the box next to **Show recent applications in Dock.**

**FaceTime High Definition Camera**

FaceTime HD Camera is the front-facing in-built web camera available on the Mac for video conferencing and to take pictures. The camera is positioned near the top edge of the Mac screen. Usually, the camera is activated automatically once you start using an app that can take pictures, record videos or make video calls like iMovie, Camera, FaceTime and others. There is a green light beside the Camera that lights up to signal that the camera is on. The light goes off when the Camera is off.

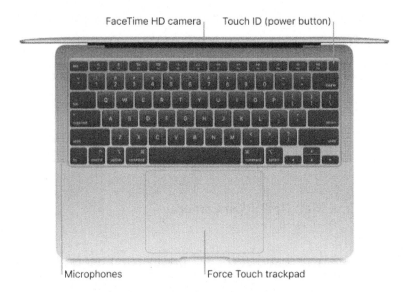

FaceTime HD camera | Touch ID (power button)

Microphones | Force Touch trackpad

**Finder**

The Finder is the gateway to locate and organize your files, apps and downloads. To access, click the **'Finder'** icon from the Dock, tap **'Command-N'** on the Keyboard or click on **Desktop > File** in the menu bar and then select **New Finder Window**. You can preview the contents of a file, rename a file, view synced devices. Also, from the **'Preview'** pane you can make use of some shortcuts to manage files from within the Finder. For example, rotating or cropping an image in MarkUp, combining images and PDF into one file. To access the preview pane in the Finder, go to **View > Show Preview**. To customize the Finder, open a **New Finder Window**, click on the **Toolbar** and then **Customize Toolbar**. Subsequently, you can add different tools such as Quick Look, Delete, Connect to an external server and Get Info to the toolbar, then click Done.

> ➢ Quick Look is to take a sneak peek at a document, photo or file in the Finder.
> ➢ Delete is to remove files and folders that you do not need any longer from the Finder.
> ➢ Connect to shared computers and servers on your network that have file sharing turned on.
> ➢ Get Info is to view information on a particular item in the Finder.

To show or hide external disks or hard disks on your desktop, go to **Finder > Preferences > General** and tick the checkboxes for the category of items you want to be displayed on your desktop. While in the **Finder > Preferences > General**, a list of options appear in the drop-down menu from which you can click on the folder that you want new Finder windows should display when it opens.


**LaunchPad**

LaunchPad is used to access (open, find and organize) your apps quickly and easily.

From the **Dock > LaunchPad icon > Click the desired app**. From the launchpad, you can also type the apps name to locate the app and press the **Return** key to open it.

To organize or move apps in the Launchpad, drag an app to a new location while to create a folder, you drag an app and place on the top of another app. To close a folder, click outside the folder and to rename a folder, open it, click on its name and type in a new name. To delete an app from Launchpad, click and hold the app until it starts shaking and then click the X sign that appears in the top-left corner of the app to conclude the deletion. If the X ign does not appear, this means the app can not be deleted. If there is ever a need to reset the Launchpad probably because new newly installed app is not being displayed there, **from Desktop > Go >**

**Press and hold the Option key and click on Library.** Open the **Application Support Folder > Dock Folder > Drag all the files with names ending with .db into the trash and then click on the Apple icon > Restart > Restart Button.** The Mac will restart and when the booting process is complete, you should be able to locate the app that was previously not being displayed. The LaunchPad organizes and arranges your apps in a grid format.

## Menu Bar

The Menu Bar is along the top of the screen and it houses icons used to manage access to Wi-Fi network, volume, launch Siri, check and monitor the battery status and the Apple menu  . The Apple menu contains prompts to lock screen, access System Preferences, shut down the computer and update Apps.

## Microphones

Microphones is used to record audio input to the computer including conference calls and music. The

3.5mm Headphone jack allows the user to listen to audio output from the Mac when a headphone or external speakers are plugged in.

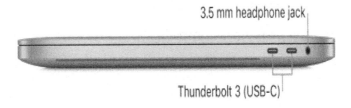

3.5 mm headphone jack

Thunderbolt 3 (USB-C)

## Notification Centre

The Notification Centre ☰ is at the top-right corner of the screen and is where you can catch up on missed email, app and reminder notifications.

To access the notification centre, click the notification centre icon. You can view notifications for that day by clicking on **'Today'**. To silence notifications so that you would not hear or see them as they come in, turn on **'Do not Disturb'**. You can also do this by going to **Apple Menu > System Preferences > Notifications.** The notifications will come in any you can view them later.

You can also manage the widgets by clicking + or – (to add or remove), click on **Edit** at the bottom of the **Today** tab and drag widget to a new location (to rearrange) and click on **Edit** and then click **App Store** (to Get More Widgets)


**Spacious Force Touch Trackpad**

The trackpad is controlled by softly sliding your fingers to control the arrow displayed on the screen and applying varying degrees of pressure to provide input to the Mac. A light press is for regular clicks while a deep press of the Trackpad is to Force Click. Depending on the App you are working on, a Force click results in different outcomes; preview (Addresses on Maps, Links in Safari or Mail, File Content), add or edit information (To add dates to a Calendar, rename a File in Finder) or to attach a file to a mail.

If your Mac is recognizing your regular clicks as force click, you need to adjust Trackpad settings by calibrating the pressure required to click your trackpad. Go to **Apple menu > System Preferences > Trackpad > 'Point and Click' > Click pressure**. Then adjust the slider on the screen to your preferred level. If you desire to switch off the Force click functionality, untick the '**Force Click and haptic feedback**' checkbox.

While at the trackpad preferences page, you can customize your gestures, know more about each gesture and customize other trackpad features.

Ensure that your Trackpad is turned on while in use as it needs power to recognize clicks and provide input to your Mac.

**Speakers system**

The Speaker is a high-fidelity sound system design to project sound output from the MacBook Air.

**Spotlight**

Spotlight provide an easy access to find things such as apps, documents, email messages, music, webpage, contacts on the MacBook Air or search for information online. It can also show calculations, movie showtimes, measurement conversions, definitions, restaurants nearby, solve equations and more.

Spotlight suggestions provides information on news, sports, movies, weather, stock market, politics and more.

Click on the search icon $\mathcal{Q}$ in the upper-right corner of the menu bar. Type in the name of what you are looking for. A results list will pop-up and you can open any item on the list while reviewing the list using the Up Arrow and Down Arrow keys. To get a list of files of the same format or type, input kind and the file type. For example, to have a list of all videos of the MacBook. Type in 'kind:video'. If the search results do not match what you are looking for, you can focus and re-direct the search results towards what you need. To customize search results, go to **System Preferences > Spotlight**. Different options with checkboxes in front of them will be displayed. Click on the Checkbox beside the category so as to define the results Spotlight will display.

To hide a content or category of contents from Spotlight search, click on the Privacy tab in the System **Preferences > Spotlight**, click on the **Add** button, next on the items you do not want Spotlight to search for and then click **Choose**.

### Thunderbolt 3 (USB-C) ports

Thunderbolt is used to connect various accessories and peripherals to the computer. The port is used to transmit data quickly (up to 40 Gb/second), charge the computer and connect to compatible displays such as projectors. The Thunderbolt 3 supports the following connections: USB, power, HDMI, VGA and DisplayPort.

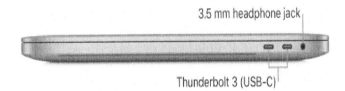

### Touch ID

The Touch ID which doubles as the power button is an electronic fingerprint reader that allows Apple device users to sign-in to their devices and authorize transactions in Apple Digital Media stores without needing to input a passcode. To configure the Touch ID, go to the **Apple menu** and select '**System Preferences**' and click on '**Touch ID**'. To add a fingerprint, click the plus sign +, input the user account password and precisely follow the instructions that pop up on the screen. You can setup a maximum of five fingerprints on your Mac but a maximum of three fingerprints per user account. To delete a fingerprint, go to the **Apple menu** and select **'System Preferences'** and click on **'Touch ID'**, put the cursor over the fingerprint icon that you intend to delete until you see the delete icon X, click on the X, enter your password and press **Delete** to commit to the deletion.

You can now select the Touch ID features you want to use on your MacBook Air. The options include unlocking your Mac, Apple Pay, iTunes store, App Store and Password Autofill. Subsequently, you can activate the Touch ID for authentication purposes by placing the finger (whose print was previously captured) gently on the Touch ID sensor.

To reboot your Mac using the Touch ID, press and hold the Touch ID button until you see the bootup screen. To switch between different user accounts on your Mac, put your finger on the Touch ID button and the Mac will return to that account corresponding to the Touch ID.

## Apps and Features of the MacBook Air 2020

Many great and wonderful apps are preloaded on the MacBook Air that will boost your productivity and help you do a wide variety of things conveniently, easier and faster. The following apps and features come right out of the box with the MacBook Air.

**Airdrop**

Airdrop enables you to send and receive documents, photos, map locations, files and webpages wirelessly (Wi-Fi and Bluetooth) to a nearby Mac, iPhone or iPad.

**Share files via Airdrop**: Just click on the item you want to send, select the **Share > Airdrop** and then recipient's device. From the Finder app, click **Airdrop** and drag the file to the recipients's device. The recipient has to choose whether or not to accept the file for the share to be completed.

**Receive files via Airdrop**: Ensure that in the AirDrop window, you have set 'Allow me to be discovered by' and choose the appropriate option (no one, contacts or everyone). Navigate to the Airdrop notification and click Accept from the pop-up menu. The file received will be added to the Downloads folder by default.

Airdrop works over Bluetooth and as such, the Bluetooth of both devices must be turned on and within 30 feet (9 metres) of each other.

**App Store**

The App Store contains all Apps compatible with the device and makes it easy for you to find, buy and install them. The apps available for download in the store have been reviewed by Apple and deemed safe and suitable for use.

To locate apps, click on the **App store** and type in word(s) relating to the app in the top- left hand corner of the Apps store window and then press '**Enter**'. A list of apps will be populated on the screen and you can then click on the apps's name or icon to see the description and view existing user ratings and reviews.

**Download and purchase apps**: To download a particular app, tap on the button that displays the price or '**Get**' and then click on the button one more time to buy the app or **install** (if the app is free). To purchase and app or an in-app content, you will need to enter your Apple ID or use your Touch ID. Sometimes, the app you wish to download have previously been purchased by other family members if you are part of a Family sharing group. While in the App store, click on your name in the bottom- left hand side of the page and a list of all apps purchased

28

using your Apple ID will be displayed. Next to download the App, click on the **'Purchased by' > family member's name > iCloud status icon beside the app.**

**Hide a purchased app**: To hide a purchased app, hold the pointer over an app, click the **'Show more'** button and then choose **Hide Purchase**. To unhide a hidden apps click on **View Information > Manage > Unhide > Done.**

**Update installed apps**: The moment an update is available for any of your downloaded Apps, a notification will be displayed in the Notifications Centre and a badge will be visible on the App store icon in the Dock (with a number displayed indicating the number of updates available). From the updates pane in the Apps store, you have the option of updating all Apps (click **Update All**) or updating individual apps (click **Update** beside each app you intend to update). You can also update an app once you receive a notification that an updated version of the apps is available or from the **Apple menu > Apps store > Updates.**

If you prefer that all your apps be automatically updated,

**App store > Preferences > Automatic Updates**

**Redownload an uninstalled app:** To reinstall a previously installed app that you uninstalled or deleted, navigate to **Apple menu > Apps store > redownload the app by clicking the redownload button.**

**Uninstall an app:** To uninstall an app, drag the app from the Applications Folder to the Trash. Once the Trash is emptied, the app is permanently removed. However, you can still get it back from the Trash before emptying by selecting **Trash > File > Put Back.** Also, from the Launchpad, hold an app till the other apps begin to move gently side to side and click the visible **Delete** button (for apps purchased from App Store).

### Apple Book

Apple Book is an app that contains books (both visual and audio) that enables you to read, listen to, arrange existing books and at the same time buy new books.

**Buy books:** Go to the **Books > Book store and type the name of a book you wish to buy.** Select a book, click on the book's price and then buy book / get book (if book is free) or pre-order. To keep a book for later, click the **Options** arrow and then **Add to Wish List**.

**Find an audiobook**: Go to **Books > AudioBook store**, after which you can buy the book gift the book after clicking the options arrow.

**Read a book**: Navigate to **Books > library** and then select the book by doubleclicking the book to open.

**Have a book read to you**: While you are doing something else you can have a book read to you. Go to **Edit > Speech > Start Speaking**. If the books comes with a **Read Aloud** feature, simply click the **Speak** button at the top of the book (in the toolbar).

**Improve the reading conditions at Night**: To improve reading conditions, choose **view > Theme and Night or Appearance > click the Black Circle.**

**Bookmark a page**: When reading a book, click the Bookmark button to ensure the page is saved and you do not lose track of the page you stopped.

**Restrict the access to certain Books:** To limit the access to a book, go to **Apple Menu > System Preferences > Screen Time > Content and Privacy** and then turn on Restrictions. Two actions can be done here; either to Disable Book Store and AudioBook store (**Apps > Deselect Books Store**) or Restrict Books with explicit content (**Stores > Deselect Explicit Books**)

**To delete a book:** Once a book is no longer required, delete the book by **Book > Library**, select the book and press the '**Delete**' key.

**Apple Mail**

Apple Mail will help you manage your emails better and faster as it offers many options for filing emails thus making its easier to search for and locate. You can send, receive and manage all your email accounts in one place using the Mail app.

**Add an email account:** Launch the **Mail** app, click **Add Account** and select the mail account type. The popular email service providers are listed for you to select from, click **Continue**, input the email address and password, click the checkboxes corresponding to the apps you would like to use with the email account and **Done..** If your email service provider is not listed, select the option **Other Mail Account**.

Choose a Mail account provider...

○ **iCloud**

○ Exchange

○ Google

○ YAHOO!

○ **Aol.**

○ Other Mail Account...

? Cancel Continue

**Stop using an email account**: Go to **Mail > Accounts** and ensure the checkbox corresponding to the mail account is not ticked. Subsequently, the emails on that account will not be shown in the **Mail** app. To resume using the email account ot view the emails on the account again, tick the checkbox corresponding to the email account.

**Remove an email account**: Go to **Mail > Preferences > Accounts,** then select the account and click **Remove.** This removal account will remove the account's emails from your Mac and they would no longer be available on your Mac. However, the emails will still be accessible and available on the server of the email service provider.

**Write and send a mail**: Click on the **New Message** button, type in the recipients in the **To** field and the **cc** field for recipients to be copied in the mail, type in the subject and body of the mail. Click the **Header** Button to include other fields such as Bcc for recipients to be blind-copied or to set the priority level of the mail. You can also use the Format button to set the font type and size, Emoji button to include emojis and symbols and Attachment button to include attachements and include your signature before sending the email.

**Read received emails**: Go to **Mail** app to see a list of received emails. You can sort (click 'Sort by') or filter your mails; by date, size, read or unread.

After reading a mail, you can choose to delete, reply or forward the email to other recipients or copy/move the mail to another mailbox by simply selecting the message and picking the desired option.

If there is an attachment included in the mail, click the attachment and click the select the **Download** option and save in the location of your choice on the Mac.

**Search for an email or Keyword**: To search for a specific email or group of emails, you can make use of criteria such as keywords in the subject or entire body of a mail or email address. Input the search criteria in the search bar, press **Return** to have a list of emails that matched the search criteria.

**Create a signature**: To create a signature, go to **Mail > Preferences> Signatures,** choose the email account for which you want to create a signature and click the **Add button +,** include a name for the signature to differentiate this signature from other signatures you may create later. On the right had side, you can create your signature and use the **Edit** menu to customize the font and layout of the text or drag an image in to add it to the signature.

**Add Signature to Email**: To automatically have the signature added to your outgoing mails, **Mail > Preferences > Signatures > Signature pop-up menu** and then select a signature. Choose **None** under the Signature pop-up menu if you do not want signatures added to sent mails automatically.
To have signatures positioned below the body of the mail you sent, ensure the checkbox for '**Place signature above quoted text**' is not ticked.
To delete the signature, **Mail > Preferences > Signatures**, select the signature and then click **Remove**.

**Block a sender**: To block a particular sender from sending emails to you, pick a previous email sent by that sender, put the cursor next to the name in the message header, click on the arrow and then select **Block Contact**. You can also block a sender by going to **Mail > Preferences > Junk Mail > Blocked > Add +.**

**Remove a sender from the blocked list:** Pick a previous email sent by that sender, put the cursor next to the name in the message header, click on the arrow and then select **Unblock** Contact. You can also unblock a sender by going to **Mail > Preferences > Junk Mail > Blocked > Remove -.**

**Other mail preferences settings** that you can customize to suit your desires include

- ➢ Font types, clour and size (Fonts and Colours)
- ➢ How messages are displayed in the Message viewer (Viewing)
- ➢ How the junk mails are treated / handled (junk email filters, blocked senders)
- ➢ Frequeny of syncing Mails app with the email service provider to fetch new messages, the sound for new message (General)

## Apple Music

Apple Music App allows you to access the world's largest music collection, listen to your collection of songs and organize the songs and albums you buy on iTunes in your personal library. Apple Music allows you to access your entire music library irrespective of whether the tracks have been downloaded or are being streamed.

**To subscribe to Apple music**: To join Apple music and be able to stream, download and manage your music playlists, launch the **Music app > Account > Join Apple music**. As a new user, you enjoy a trial period during which you do not have to pay any fees. However, a monthly subscription fee would apply once the trial period is over. Once you buy or download music, it is updated in your music library and any song that is not in already in the Store is added to iCloud.

**Add music to your library**: To add download music to your Mac, launch the Music app, search the Music catalog (input a keyword that relates to the song in the search field) and click **Apple music** option. When you see the song of your choice in the search results, select the **More** button next to it and **Add to library** or **Download**. Dowloading a song allows you have access to it even when you are offline (not connected to the internet).

You can also view recommendations of songs that were curated for you based on your listening history and preferences and **What's new** to find new songs.

**Listen to Songs**: To play songs, launch the music app, navigate to the song you wish to listen to, click on it and **Play** or Click on the song. You can use the controls to pause, repeat, play songs in a defined order or shuffle songs.

**Share music library with others**: You can share with other users that you authorize to (with a password), **System preferences > Sharing > Media sharing > Share media with guests > Choose the items you wish to share (All songs, movies and TV shows or Selected playlists).** If you intend to stop sharing at any time, **System preferences > Sharing > Media sharing** and deselect the checkbox for **Share media with guests.**

**Apple Pay**

Apple Pay is a contactless payment and digital wallet technology for Apple devices that enables you make easy and secure payments for purchases on your Mac.

**Configure Apple Pay**: To setup Apple Pay if you did not set it up during your first start-up of the Mac, go to the Apple menu, select 'System Preferences', click on 'Wallet and Apple Pay' and then 'Add Credit or Debit Card to fill in the required information for verification by your Bank.

**Pay for purchases with Apple Pay**: Once you have setup Apple Pay, the next time you are prompted to or see Apple Pay as a payment option on a website, the merchant's details (name and purchase amount) will be visible on the screen. Confirm that the billing, shipping and other information is valid (if the information is not available or invalid, input the required information) and correct. Next, put your finger on the Touch ID to authenticate and complete the purchase successfully. Please note that Apple Pay is not available in all countries or regions of the World. Kindly visit the Apple website for an updated list of eligible locations.

**Apple TV**

The Apple TV app allows you to buy, rent and watch all your favourite movies and TV shows from any of your devices.

**Search for Content**: You can browse for content by clicking the Movies, TV shows, or Kids tab in the menu and then pick the genre and look through. When you find content you wish to watch, you have the option of buying or renting. You can also share with up to six Family members through Family sharing.

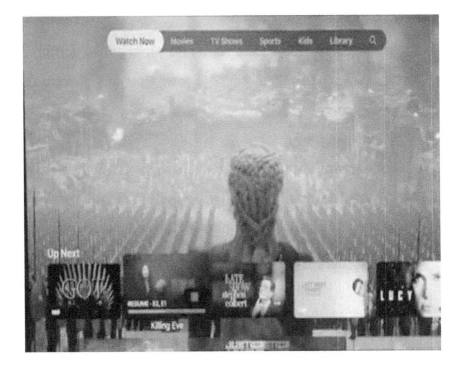

**Watch Now** is a broad collection of content recommended to you based on the movies and TV shows you are subscribed to or watched.

**UpNext** contains movies or TV shows you have added to your queue or watching. To add a new movie to UpNext, click the **Add to Up Next button**. Contents that you have started watching or plan to watch are displayed in the Up Next Row. To add a content to Up Next, in the Watch Now list, click **Add to Up Next**.

**Play or watch a movie**: To play a movie or watch a show, Launch the Apple TV app, select the option Wach Now, browse through content available (recommended TV shows), select an item and click **Play**. Ou can only play free items or items you have previously bought or subscribed for. To buy or rent a movie, click on an item and select the option Buy or Rent.

You can customize the settings to suit your preference. Options like Always check for available downloads, automatic downloads, checkboxes in library and list size.

**Calendar**

Calendar is a great way to keep your schedule organized and ensure you do not miss any important events or appointments. Alert notifications are also sent when the event is due.

**Create an event**: To create an event, go to calendars and tap the + sign. Input the Title of the Event, location, start and end time including travel time. When you add a location (with address or landmark) to an event, a map and weather information are also added. The map will help inform you of the directions to the location. (you can edit an existing event to view event details and Add Location).

**Invite contacts to Calendar events**: You can invite people to calendar events provided their email addresses are in your Contacts/Mails App/ Calendar servers and they use the same calendar service provider as you are. Click on the event and then select **Add invitees**. Enter each invitees name or email address and press Return once the Calendar has matched the invitee details you input in the Contacts and Mail Apps and then click send.

**Change the Calendar Views**: You can toggle the calendar view between day, week, month and year.

**Create Multiple Calendars**: You can also create separate calendars, each for a different purpose. From **Calendar App, select file > new calendar** and the account for the calendar and assign a name to the calendar.

**Delete an existing Calendar**: To delete an existing calendar, from the calendar app, **view > show calendar list > edit** and then **Delete**. While on the show calendar list page, you can show or hide a calendar's events (by ticking or unticking the checkbox in the calendar list) and show or hide events from all calendars (by ticking or unticking the checkbox in the calendar list). Click on a coloured circle to choose any colour for a calendar from the show calendar list and all the colour of the events for that calendar will change.

**Connecting to the internet**
Connecting to the internet on your MacBook Air can generally be done in three ways namely Wi-Fi, Ethernet or Instant Hotspot.

**Connect to the Internet via Wi-Fi:** Using Wi-Fi, click on the Wi-Fi option, choose a network and then click Join to access the Wi-Fi network of your choice (if the network is locked, you will be required to input the password before you can gain access). You can turn off or turn on the Wi-Fi by choosing Turn Wi-Fi On or Turn Wi-Fi Off in the menu bar.

**Connect to the Internet via Ethernet:** Use an ethernet cable to connect a modem or router to the ethernet port of your Mac. You may require a Thunderbolt to Gigabit Ethernet adapter if there are compatibility challenges. Go to **System Preferences > Network > Ethernet > Confgure IPv4 > the preferred configuration method of your Internet Service Provider (ISP) from the list (Using DHCP or using BootP, Using DHCP with manual address or Manually) > Advanced > DNS > Add + > Input the IP address of the DNS Server of your ISP > OK.** Once the settings have been configured correctly, the Ethernet service will be activated..

**FaceTime**

Facetime is used to make phone calls either to one person or to a group of people (up to 32). FaceTime calls can only be made to others who also have a Mac, iOS or iPadOS devices that have an active internet connection.

**Sign into and Sign out from FaceTime:** Launch the FaceTime app enter your Apple ID, password and click

Sign in. To sign out from FaceTime, select FaceTime > Preferences and click Sign out from the Settings.

**Make a FaceTime call**: To make a FaceTime call, go to the FaceTime app, sign in with your Apple ID, input the email address or phone number of the person you want to speak with and press Return (repeat this step if you intend to speak with multiple people until they have all been added). Next, click the Video or Audio button to start the FaceTime call. During the call, you can pause the call, mute, increase or decrease the call volume. If the recipient did not pick the call or declined, click **Message** to drop a text message for the person if you are both signed into iMessage.

**Signed into FaceTime but not to receive Calls**: Once you are signed out of FaceTime, you will be unable to receive calls until you are signed in again.

If you wish to remain signed into FaceTime but do not want to receive FaceTime calls, you can turn off FaceTime To turn off ot Turn on FaceTime, go to FaceTime > Turn FaceTime Off or Turn FaceTime On.

**Block a Caller**: To avoid FaceTime calls with particular individuals, you can block them on all your devices by going to FaceTime > Preferences > Blocked and clicking the Add Button + and selecting the names of the people to be blocked from your list of contacts. When a contact is blocked, if they call you, you would not receive any notifications and the call will not be answered.

**Other FaceTime Preference settings**: You can customize the FaceTime settings to suit your needs in the preferences tab. This allows you to set your preferred setting regarding Allowing your Mac to use your iPhone to make and receive calls, Ringtones and Allowing Capture of Live Photos during Video calls.

**Find My**

Find My is a feature useful for locating a missing device, family and friends who have shared their location with you even when the devices is not connect to WiFi.

**Share your location with friends and family**: You can share location with friends by following the path, **people**

**list > Share My Location and define the time period you want the Sharing to last for**. You can also automatically share alerts to family and friends to notify them when you arrive a particular location.

**Find a stolen or lost device**: To locate a missing device, first you must add the device in the '**Find My**' app. Next, go to the devices list and select the device you want to locate. If the device can be located, it will appear on the map. You can click the Info button on the map, then Directions which opens the Maps app and shows the directions from your location to the device's current location.

On the info button, you can also chose the option to play sound a device on your list. If the device is online, the sound starts playing but if the device is offline, the sound starts playing when the device is within range (airpods) or starts playing when the device gets connected to a Wi-Fi or cellular network.

If the device can not be located, a message stating that 'no location found' appears below the device's name.

However, the option to 'notify when found' can be selected if you click the Info button ⓘ on the map.

**Activation lock:** The lock is activated once the **Find My** feature is turned on to prevent anyone else from accessing or using your Mac if it ever gets stolen or missing. Activation lock will ensure that before **Find My** is turned off, device deactivated or data on the device erased, the input of Apple ID and password is required.

**GarageBand**

GarageBand is a music studio apps that can be used to create, record and share your own music. The app is fitted with notepad, Apple loops, smart controls and editors that will enable you to add loops, learn how to play an instrument, write music, arrange and mix your music and record any sound that can be picked up by a microphone. Once completed, you can share to iTunes, iCloud, SoundCloud or to other devices.

**Record a new music project:** Launch **Garageband, choose Track > New Track,** select microphone, the triangle beside the Details tab to customize your desired

options for input, output and monitoring the recording
and then click Create and the Record button.

**Drummer beat and other loops**: You can add a drummer
beat by dragging a drummer loop into the empty portion
of the Tracks area in the loop Browser. GarageBand has
a collection of software instruments (pianos, keyboards,
guitars,, horns and other instruments) to use in creation
of your music projects.

**Instrument lessons:** There are in-built lessons on how to play guitar or piano that you can play along with the teacher while watching the teacher's instruction. GarageBand provides you with your own home recording studio on your Mac.

### Handoff

The Handoff feature enables you to continue on another device where you stopped on another device.

**Continuity with Handoff:** Once you are logged into the MacBook Air, iOS deVice or iPadOS devices with the same Apple ID and WiFi and Bluetooth is enabled, an icon will apepar in the Dock whenever an activity is being handed off.. You can be checking out information on a webpage on your MacBook Air and Handoff to your iPhone to pick up where you have left off. Handoff works with a lot of Apple Apps but the devices involved must meet certain system requirements. To turn Handoff on, go to System Preferences > General > Allow Handoff this Mac and your iCloud devices.

**Turn off Handoff**: To turn Handoff off, go **to System Preferences > General > Allow Handoff this Mac and your iCloud devices** but select deselect the option '**Allow Handoff this Mac and your iCloud devices**'.

### iCloud

The iCloud contains files in the iCloud drive and Photos in the iCloud Photos to optimize space on your Mac. The iCloud is useful for storage of content ranging from books to photos, contacts, apps, music to documents and movies. Anything stored on iCloud and be accessed from any Apple or Internet enabled device with a supported browser. Once a file is moved to iCloud, it leaves behind a lower quality version or icon of that file so that when next you want to access the file, just click on the file and it will downloaded back to the Mac when its connected to the Internet.

**Turn iCloud features on or Off**: To turn on iCloud, go to Apple menu, then System Preferences > Sign in with your Apple ID > iCloud > Click the checkbox for apps you intend whose iCloud features you intend to use apps.

With the same navigation path, you can ensure that the checkbox that corresponds to any app whose iCloud features you do not intend to use is not ticked.

**Back up to iCloud**: To include these files in back up for the iCloud drive, go to **Apple Menu > System Preferences > Apple ID > iCloud and uncheck the option for Optimize Mac Storage**. For iCloud Photos, go to **Photos > Preferences > Download Originals to this Mac**. The contents of the iCloud drive and Photos will then be stored on the Mac and in the Back Up.

You can also share photos and albums, locations and calendar with users that you choose using the iCloud. Furthermore, iCloud can be used to locate your MacBook Air if the device goes missing.

**iMovie**

The iMovie app is a video app that enables you to record, watch, edit and share movies on your Mac. You can create movies, create trailers and video effects to the content you created. When the movie is completed, you

can share to other devices or send it to the Apple TV
App.

**Create a movie project**: To create a movie project, click
**Create + > Movie,** all the photos and videos you have in
your media library is displayed. Select the files (a tick
sign would be displayed on the selected files) you want
to include in your movie and then click Create Movie at
the bottom of the screen.

**Edit a movie**: After creating a movie, you may edit the
movie to add photos, music, sound effects or a

voiceover to it. Open the movie, click the Add Media button and add the file to your movie.

**Add video to iMovie Project**: To record a video and include in an iMovie project, click the Add media button, Camera and then the Record button to commence recording the video. When completed, tap the Record button to stop recording, the Pay button to preview the video and Use vide to add the video to your movie project or Retake to trash the recorded vieo and make a new recording.

**Add photos to an iMovie project**: To take and include photos in an iMovie project, , click the Add media button, Camera and change from the Video mode to Photo mode to take a photo.. Tap Use Photo to add the photo to include the photo in the project or Retake to take a new photo and discard the existing photo.

**Create trailers**: To create trailers, click the New button, trailer a Trailer template of your choice and then create. Upon completion, you can edit to include some information to the trailer like movie name, title, cast members and credits.

Always ensure you have enough space before commencing a new project to avoid running out of space during filming or production of the movie.

**Keynote**

The Keynote app is used to create professional, world-class presentations on your Mac. The app has preloaded themes that makes it easy for you to create and improve your presentations.

You can add text, objects, pictures, animations, videos and select colours of your choice. Once completed, you can share the work to other devices, on social media or in a mail.

**Create a presentation**: To create a presentation, click on **File > New > select a theme** and click the Add Button + to add a slide.

**Practice the presentation**: To practice your presentation and view the slides and a timer to ensure you do not run out of time during the actual presentation, select Play >

Rehearse Slideshow. Practice makes perfect.

**Share presentation slides**: To share the presentation,

select the **presentation > Share > Send a copy.**

**Maps**

Maps is an app that would help you view and get

directions to various places/locations using Satellite

imagery. Maps will provide information on how to

navigate to different place, get advice on the best routes

using different means of transportation, real-time traffic

information and voice navigation.

**Get Direction**: Type in the **start** and **end** locations and

then click **Directions** to find the best route to your

destination with option of **Drive, Walk** or **Transit** (click

the **Share** button to send the directions to your iPhone,

iPad  or other iOS device with the same Apple ID signed

in and be guided to your destination by the voice

prompts).

**View routes and transit suggestions:** Click Transit for the app to provide you with suggestions on travel options and approximate travel times. You can View Direction for an alternate route and click on Details for the preferred route, Zoom in on a step and Choose when to leave or arrive to get the best ideas on using public transport based on the real-time transit schedules. The app also provides contact details for places like hotels and restaurants including reviews by people who have previously visited the location.

**Messages**

The Messages app allows you to send and receive unlimited texts, photos, video to and from anyone with a Mac, iPad, iPhone or iPod Touch.

# iMessage

Sign in with your Apple ID
to activate iMessage.

Learn more about iMessage

| | |
|---|---|
| Apple ID | example@icloud.com |
| Password | required |

Sign In...

Forgot Apple ID or Password?

Create New Apple ID

**Setup Messages**: To setup Messages, launch the App from your desktop or the Dock and input your Apple ID and password. Click on messages in the menu bar and choose **Preferences > Accounts** and input the phone number and email addresses you would like to be reached on. Also, select the phone number and email address that will be displayed when you are using the

63

Messages app, whether you want Read Receipts to be sent to senders for messages you have read and whether you want messages to be stored in iCloud. Once you are signed in, you can send unlimited texts, videos and photos with other Apple users (Mac, iPhone, iPod or Apple Watch)

**Send a message:** Launch the **Messages** app, click on **Compose** and input the name, email address or phone number in the field indicated **To**. You can also add the intended recipient from your Contact list. Type in the body of the message, drag and drop or copy and paste any media file (photos or videos) to be inserted into the message and press **Return** to send the message.

**Forward a message:** Go to the Messages app, click on the message to highlight it and choose the option **Forward,** include a recipient name, email address or phone number and press **Return.**

**Delete a message:** Launch the Messages app, open the message to be deleted, click on The white area around the message, select **Delete** and click **Delete.**

For audio or video calls, make use of FaceTime.

**Optimize Space on MacBook Air**

Sometimes space can be a premium. Therefore, to free up space on the Computer and leave space for other content and make the device run smoothly, the storage space has to be optimized. Some of the methods to approach storage optimization (Apple Menu > About this Mac > Storage > Manage) are outlined below.

> ➢ Make less use of the storage space on the Mac by storing all files, messages and Photos in iCloud. Doing this does not limit access to the files as you can still access the files exactly where they are located on the MacBook Air.
>
> ➢ Store movies and TV shows in the Apple TV app and remove the contents you downloaded but have watched.
>
> ➢ Delete items that have stayed longer than 30 days automatically from the Trash.
>
> ➢ Regularly take stock to identify large unwanted files and delete them.

**Safari**

Safari is the native browser with which you can browse the internet on your MacBook Air.

**Visit a website**: To visit a website, launch Safari from the Dock, input the website's address in the address bar at the top of the page and press Return on the Keyboard.

**Run a web search**: If you do not have a website in mind but wish to run a search, in the address bar, input the keyword or query and press Return.

**Bookmark a website**: If you would like to bookmark the website you have visited for ease of future reference, press **Command + D** on your Keyboard and type in a title for the bookmark or leave as is and click **Add**. To view a list of bookmarked pages, click the Show Sidebar button and select the Bookmarks tab. If you wish to remove a bookmarked page, click on Bookmarks in the menu bar and Edit Bookmarks. Click on the Bookmark and Delete.

**Homepage:** To make a website the Safari Homepage, go to the General tab of the Safari and input the website in the space provided for Homepage or click Set to Current Page.

**Share website with friends:** To share a website with friends and family, go the the top right of thr Safari window and click **the Share Sheet Button > Sharing method** (Email, Airdrop, Notes, Reminders or any third party app that is applicable)

**Private Browsing:** You can visit web pages without saving cookies or storing your search history or AutoFill information. This is especially useful when searching for flights or shopping. Click on **File** in the Safari menu bar and **New Private Window** or **Shift+Command+N**.
To view a web page devoid of the animations originally programmed into the page, you can click the Reader View button which is located to the left of the address bar. Various options are available to customize the Reader View to suit the user including changing the font

& size, changing the background colour, click on the Reader Options button and select the settings of your choice.

**Screen Time**

Screen Time is a tool that helps you monitor time spent in apps and websites with the MacBook Air. With this, you have insights into your usage trends and can then put in place controls and limits to regulate the time spent using specific activities and view reports for you or your children.

**Turn on screen time**: You can turn on screen time by selecting **Apple menu > System Preferences > Screen Time > Options > Turn On**. Next, you can Share across devices if you want Screen Time reports to include time spent on other devices with the same Apple ID signed in and Use Screen Time Passcode to put additional level of security on access to the Screen Time settings (to request for a password to allow additional time when the time limits has passed).

**Set limits and restrictions**: You can use downtime (time away from the screen), App Limits (set limits for the amount of time spent in specific apps, types of apps and websites) and Apps that are always allowed(even during scheduled Downtimes).

**Screen Time reports**: View Screen Time Reports gives insights into the following

- ➢ App Usage includes charts that display app usage and you can filter the view to show statistics for a specific time period, app category, website or device.
- ➢ Notifications includes charts that indicate the number of times your receive notifications.
- ➢ Pickups includes charts that reveal the number of times to use it and the very first app you use.

**Sidecar**

Sidecar is a continuity feature enables you to use iPad in a landscape orientation as a secondary display for your Mac or a writing/drawing pad and extend your workspace.

This will enable you to pair your ipad with Apple Pencil and whatever actions you take will be reflected on the Mac.

**To activate Sidecar**: To use this feature, Wi-Fi and Bluetooth must be turned on and certain system requirements must be met. You also need to be logged into the same iCloud account on both devices and then go to **Apple menu > System Preferences > Sidecar**

**Siri**

Siri is the voice and text controlled virtual assistant developed by Apple and made available on its devices that can answer questions, carry out commands and access other applications. Siri can play music, manage files, send messages, assist to place calls and manage your calendar.

**Activate Siri**: To get Siri going, go to **'system Preferences'**, click on **'Siri'**, select **'Enable Ask Siri'**

(deselect the checkbox to stop using Siri) and then **'Listen for Hey Siri'**.

**Invoke Siri**: You can either invoke—Siri by saying **'Hey Siri'** or using buttons.

You can also interact with Siri via text by typing your request **'Type to Siri'. System Preferences > Accessibility > Siri and Enable Type to Siri.** You can also take the following actions to ask Siri: Click the Siri icon from the menu bar or dock or Press and hold the **Command + Space bar** until Siri responds

**Amend or edit Siri commands:** To make amendments on a command already passed to Siri, click on the words in the Siri window, make the required changes and press Return.

You can also customize Siri and select your preferences for Language, dialect and Voice, Apps that Siri can learn from, allow Siri when your Mac is locked, show Siri in menu bar and turn voice feedback on or off.

**System Preferences**

System Preferences is where your preferred settings on MacBook Air is personalized. You can get there by either clicking on the System Preferences icon in the Dock or Apple Menu > System Preferences and then selecting the Preference you want to customize.

**Transfer and Restore Data from another Mac or PC to the new Mac**

Transfer and Restore Data from another Mac or PC to the new Mac can be easy and seamless with the use of ethernet cables and adapters, USB storage device or wirelessly.

**Copy from using a USB storage device:** To copy from using a USB storage device, connect the device to the Mac using the USB-C to USB Adapter and then drag and drop the files from the storage device to the MacBook.

**Wireless Transfer:** To transfer wirelessly, follow the on-screen instructions using the setup assistant during the initial setup or the migration assistant to transfer data afterwards. Go to the **applications folder > Utilities**

**Assistant > Migration Assistant,** click **Continue,** select the applicable option from the list (Transfer from a Mac, Time Machine Back Up or StartUp Disk) and click **Continue.** If required to input a security code, make sure the code is accurate. Next, select the information to transfer snd click **Continue to initiate the Transfer.** The two computers have to be connected to the same network and in close proximity to each other during the data migration.

Time machine is the built-in feature backs up everything on your MacBook Air which allows you to restore your MacBook Air incase anything happens to the device. When you have backup, you can restore files from your backup in the event that the original files are deleted, erased or missing . Activate the Time Machine by connecting the external storage device to the MacBook Air either through Wi-Fi or cable. From **system preferences > Time Machine > Back Up Automatically** and then select the preferred BackUp drive.

**True Tone with Retina Display**

True Tone with Retina Display is a feature that auto-adapts the display color of the device to be sin sync with the light of the environment you are in. You can set your TrueTone settings by going to **Apple Menu > System Preferences > Displays > True Tone.**

**MacOS Catalina**

MacOS 10.15 Catalina is the newest operating System for the Mac. Catalina is an upgrade from the previous version macOS 10.14 Mojave and is packed with so many useful features that would make for an awesome update. The update is free just like previous Apple software updates.

**macOS Catalina Compatible devices**: If you use any of the devices below or already have the macOS Mojave installed, get your hands on the latest macOS Catalina.

- Mac (2015 and later)
- Mac Air (2012 and later)
- Mac (2012 and later)
- Mac Mini (2012 and later)
- iMac (2012 and later)
- iMac Pro (2017 and later)
- Mac Pro (2013 and later)

**Upgrade to macOS Catalina**: Once you make the decision to upgrade to Catalina and you have (or can have) free space up to 12.5 GB of storage space, connect an external storage device to the Mac and select the device as the backup disk. You should be automatically prompted to choose **Encrypt Backup Disk** and then **Use as Backup Disk**. If you did not receive a prompt, go to **System Preferences > Time Machine > Select Backup Disk** and then pick the newly connected external storage device from the list of disks displayed on the screen. Next, choose **Encrypt Backup Disk** and then **Use as Backup Disk.** Time Machine will make commence the backup and provide you with progress reports. Upon completion of the backup, navigate to **System Preferences > Software Update** or visit the **App Store** to download and install the update.

**Changes and Improvements in the macOS Catalina**

> ➤ **Notes App** ⸺ has new sharing options that allows you to share a note or a collection of notes either giving the recipient either a view only right ot ability to edit.
> ➤ **Quick Multitasking** to switch in between apps. Once you put the cursor over the green button on any app, the option to tile it to the left or right

appears which would allow you to send the app to another side of the screen so you can open another app next to it.

➢ **Appending signature to Documents** with your iPhone or iPad  on PDF or other documents using the Markup menu inside the Preview, choose signature and create signature. You can also use Preview to edit images (resize, annotate or change the file type)

➢ **Sharing iCloud Files** with other users can be done by clickin on the folder and choosing the share option.

➢ **iTunes exists no more** and gives way to new MacOS apps ; Apple Music, Apple TV and Apple Podcasts.

➢ **Apple Podcasts** makes it easy for users who have affinity for podcasts to manage the podcast library, find and view contents by topic, title or the newly introduced editor categories.

➢ **Safari Browser** comes with a startup page that allows you access **Favourites** faster and incorporates suggestions made by Siri to surface frequently visited websites, bookmarks and iCloud tabs.

➢ **Find My app** helps you locate your Mac if it goes missing, friends and family. The Find My app is a combination of Find My iPhone and Find My Friends into one app.

➢ Hit 'Command + Option+ Escape' keys to force-close tasks, 'Command + Delete' to delete files, 'Command + Shift + 3' to screenshot the entire screen, 'Function + F5' for a list of synonyms to a word while typing.

➢ **The Photos app** intelligently features your best photos and removes poor quality photos and duplicates. Also, pictures are organized by day, month and year for ease of access.

➢ **Automatically turn on dark mode** at a particular time of the day. The dark mode makes the user interface into a black or deep-grey shade that makes it easier to use the device in dark or low light environments. Go to **system preferences > General > Appearance > Auto**

78

- ➤ **Sidecar** is the continuity feature enables you to use iPad in a landscape orientation as a secondary display for your Mac or a writing/drawing pad and extend your workspace. This implies that you can use Apple Pencil to draw, make designs and sketches, edit pictures or bring 3D models to life on your iPad and use the content real-time on your Mac.

- ➤ **Screen Time** is a tool that helps you monitor time spent in apps and websites with the Mac. With this, you have insights into your usage trends. Communication limitsa allows you to determine contacts that your children can interact with even during downtimes.

- ➤ **Apple Mails** app has a new feature enabling users to block unwanted emails from particular senders, removing your email from the suscription list of unsolicited commercial ad emails.

- ➤ **32-bit apps need to be updated to 64-bit** before they can work on the macOS Catalina. You will be prompted to install the updates.

**Safety, Use and Care information for the MacBook Air**

Apple Produts have a reputation of being very well designed to world-class standards for safety of the device. A good understanding and frequent reference when in doubt and strict adherence to the following safety instructions is recommended to ensure you extract maximum benefit and safe usage.

- The MacBook Air setup should be done on a flat stable surface.
- At all times, ensure the MacBook is kept far away from all forms of liquid (dironks, drinking water,

shower, bathtubs). If water spills on the device, it may get damaged.

- Disconnect the power plug by pulling at the plug, not the cord.
- During usage, the base of the MacBook usually gets warm. Therefore, do not place on your laps for a long period as it may cause you to have a burn.
- Connectors are supposed to fit into ports with ease. Do not force a connector into any port. If a connector does not fit into a port easily, it probably was not meant to fit into that port.
- There are airflow vents are the base of the MacBook Air designed to ensure the device does not overheat. Therefore, it would be imperative that the device is not placed on any material that can block the airflow vents.
- Before cleaning the outer parts of the device or the screen, shut down the MacBook Air and unplug the power adapter. Please use a soft, damp (with water) cloth or cotton and avoid using aerosols, sprays or abrasive material.

- The battery is screwed in at the rear of the device. Do not attempt to remove and/or replace the battery by yourself for any reason. The battery should be replaced by Authorized Apple Products Service provider or Apple Engineer. Also, protect the device from heat sources (above 100°c) as the battery may be inflammed. Operating temperatures within the range of of 10°c to 35°c and storage temperature of -25°c to 45°c are recommended.

- Use a compact bag or briefcase to carry your MacBook around. If there are other items in the bag, please ensure that they are well arranged and incapable of damaging the device.

- Please visit Apple repair centre or Service Centres Authorized by Apple) for any servicing or repairs that require disassembling the device. Unauthorized servicing or opening of the device may void the warranty.

- Avoid exposure to high volumes when playing a media file with the device. High volumes may lead to hearing impairment.